For David

thanks for many
years of kindness

David W. Beer

PIECES OF THE PAST

PIECES OF THE PAST

A RECOLLECTION

DAVID W. BEER

Lexington Avenue Books

NEW YORK

ISBN: 978-0-578-30673-5

*Title-page image of David W. Beer in
New York City, 2014*

. . .

Picture research by Laurie Platt Winfrey

Book design by Barbara M. Bachman

Printed in Mexico

TO MY WONDERFUL CHILDREN,

Elizabeth and Andrew.

..

AND TO THE MEMORY

OF MY BELOVED

Tyree.

CONTENTS

CONTENTS

PIECES OF THE PAST

PREFACE

I HAVE NOT ATTEMPTED TO PROVIDE A DETAILED ACCOUNT of my professional or personal life in these pages. Instead, I have set out to write about the things, the people, the moments that I have treasured, some significant, others not, and to re-create as much as I can of a past that is rapidly receding—indeed, in the world to come after the changes wrought by the pandemic, it may vanish altogether. The people I have loved are in here, and so are the places that have given me joy.

Although I left the practice of architecture seven years ago, the practice has not left me. Every night while trying to get to sleep, my mind ponders the design problems that I encountered years ago, desperately searching for solutions that eluded me way back then. Happily, my daydreaming is decidedly less feverish. I muse that I should have been more monk-like, more dedicated to my profession. Maybe I should have spent less time gyrating to the beat of the cha-cha on the quay of the island of Hydra, or romping with a batch of demi-royals in ornate

Hydra 1959. I worked in Athens, but played on the island of Hydra, where we would go in a large group on weekends.

Venetian palazzos on the Grand Canal. Such machinations did not further my career any more than windmill-sighting from high up on Mount Parnassus garnered me even a bit of a Pritzker Prize. Still, the thought of those times makes me smile.

Now in 2021 we are slowly emerging from a long lockdown due to the coronavirus. Over this last year I have had time to recall events that have remained vivid since I first climbed up to the upper deck of an open-air Fifth Avenue bus in my progressive West Village neighborhood and traveled to the hushed and oh-so-gracious world of my grandparents' largish house on East 74th Street. My life has continued to straddle two worlds. I have thoroughly enjoyed them both, whether at a simple taverna by the sea on a Greek island or at a much-prized table by a window at The Restaurant at the Ritz in London. In the French that I regrettably never quite mastered in all the fine schools I attended, I begin this remembrance with a heartfelt:

Vive la différence!

—DAVID W. BEER,
NEW YORK CITY

PLACES

MY ELDERLY RELATIONS DID NOT HAVE COUNTRY houses, they had places. The one I remember best was Aunt Elsie and Uncle Leo's place in Dobbs Ferry. Located high on a hill and reached by a circular drive bordered by copper beeches, it was a rather rambling house from which you could see the distant Hudson. Off the deeply shaded porch was a large swimming pool where the children played while the grown-ups partook of a proper lunch served by a white-uniform-wearing Irish maid. I easily accepted this as the way most elderly relatives lived—Aunt Alice had two such places in nearby Hartsdale, one clad with stone for the winter, another with wood clapboard for the summer. The properties were connected by a plot of land devoted to a tennis court used in the afternoon for guests of my parents' age who played doubles, always dressed appropriately in white. In Ossining, Uncle Arthur's place boasted a natural-seeming swimming pool, the water for which was supplied by a

The Nathan sisters, Irma and Bella, dressed in their fin de siècle finery. Once they were married, they lived in two houses next to each other on East 74th Street.

Left: My grandparents Frank
and Marie Wells Fay lived in
Greenville, Pennsylvania.
He founded the town's principal
industry and became a state
senator and college president.

Above: Hartsdale, before the
summerhouse porch. The maid
atop wore white.

Looking toward
the Hudson past
the copper beeches
in Dobbs Ferry.

waterfall fed from the hill above. It was especially appealing to us kids. In Tarrytown, Aunt Marjorie, acknowledged by one and all to have the most exquisite taste, had a place filled with subtly shaded chintzes that shimmered brightly when the sun shone through the partially shrouded windows.

Still farther out of town, and located on a much higher hill than the others, stood Aunt Irma's place in Mount Kisco. Early on I understood why she lived more graciously than the rest. One year, she arranged for me to watch the Macy's Thanksgiving Day Parade from the store's fourth-floor balcony. She and her husband, Jesse, spelled their last name *Straus* with only one *s*, and it appeared that he owned Macy's. It was then that their visible means of support became obvious to me. Aunt Irma was my grandmother's sister, allowing my grandmother to have a Macy's credit card numbered "2," which I would kill for now, status-conscious crumb that I am.

The Walter E. Beer Jr.'s did not have a place in the country. My grandfather quite famously said that he could drink just as easily in the city as in the country, and so on most Sundays we climbed atop the Fifth Avenue double-decker bus to travel north, leaving behind our 1930s liberal world of the West Village for my grandparents' five-story house on 74th Street between Madison and Park. Although we were lunching in the city and not Dobbs Ferry, we still had Winnifred in white to serve a proper lunch of jellied madrilène topped with sour cream, roast beef or a capon, usually followed by crème brûlée. My brother and I ate with the grown-ups. A good thing, too, as

*395 Bleecker
Street.
The Bleecker
Gardens
behind made
it special.*

the food was absolutely delicious. Incidentally, although martinis were enthusiastically served, no wine was poured, which on
reflection seems a bit odd since before the First World War my
grandfather dragged my grandmother, my father, and his sisters
to Paris for a year while he studied French law, which hardly led
to a very lucrative career. He devoted his life to charity, without
leaving his grandson a sum that might have allowed me to stay
at the Plaza Athénée much later in life.

　　In the family, Grandfather's charity was referred to as Fed-

eration, always Federation, never the Federation of Jewish Phi-
lanthropies. It wasn't until I was fourteen that it began to dawn
on me that the one thing that all my relatives had in common,
besides their country places, was they were all Jewish. Before
that, how was I to know? Aunt Elsie and Uncle Leo, the ones
with the copper-beech-lined circular driveway up to the house

*49 and 51 East 74th Street. The houses that Jesse Straus
and Walter Beer built for their families.*

Florence and Wally Beer. Their apartment in Brooklyn Heights had a fabulous view of the New York Harbor.

that faced the Hudson, annually held a legendary Christmas party replete with an elaborately trimmed tree whose top scraped their apartment's ceiling. True, my father swore that he would never buy a German car, but then that view was quite common among fathers in those days. When one of my relatives had the misfortune to leave behind an exceedingly com-

fortable existence, my parents would bid them a fond farewell
at Frank Campbell's. Very secular Saturday mornings found my
father at his desk on Wall Street, bent over a legal brief, certainly not over his morning Sabbath prayers. Growing up, our

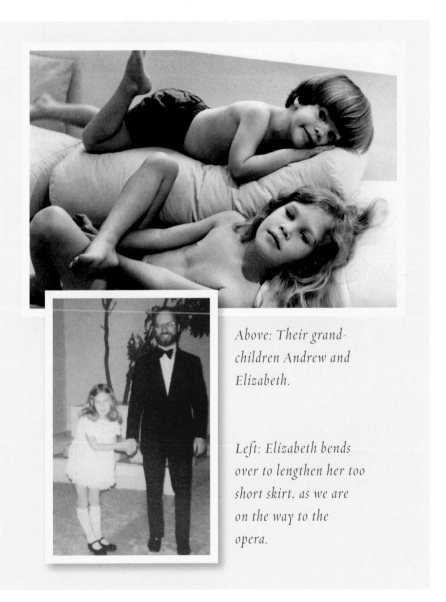

Above: Their grand-
children Andrew and
Elizabeth.

Left: Elizabeth bends
over to lengthen her too
short skirt, as we are
on the way to the
opera.

mother belonged to a variety of Protestant churches, switching as we changed neighborhoods. Her own father was Frank L. Fay. He barely missed being born in County Cork, as his parents arrived here just in time to give birth to him in this country. Given her Irish background, you might have assumed that her church-going would be of a more serious nature than occasionally attending Madison Avenue Presbyterian, where I sang in the children's choir. Badly.

It was not until my freshman year at Exeter in 1948 that my Jewish heritage became known to me and, as it turned out, to others. In the school production of the 1930s farce, *Boy Meets Girl,* I played a female stenographer, rather too realistically I fear. My classmate Tim Cogan, appraising my appearance, exclaimed, "You certainly do look Jewish!" If the shoe fits . . . Soon after, when I started spending weekends on the North Shore of Long Island, my friend's parents would tell their daughter how liberal they were to take me to the Piping Rock Club in Locust Valley. That gesture was perhaps the only liberal one they made, since they all still hated Roosevelt, a fact that they reminded me of almost hourly.

Just after my senior year at Harvard, I was invited to a wedding in Palm Beach along with my friend Elizabeth Berlin, the composer's daughter, with the idea, I suppose, that we could lounge together on the very public beach while the other out-of-town guests frolicked on the properly restricted beach of the Bath and Tennis Club. When Elizabeth ultimately canceled, what were they to do? I could not play on the beach all by myself.

Soon, I, too, was frolicking in the Addison Mizner splendor of the B&T and dining exclusively at the Everglades Club, unaware of the turmoil I was causing. It was not until much later that I learned the powers that be had held a special meeting to find a solution to the serious situation thrust upon them. One gentleman was heard to say, "But we did not even let Bernard Baruch in."

Still later, I finally read *Our Crowd,* Stephen Birmingham's well-researched history on German Jews in America, and began to appreciate my heritage. I recalled that my grandparents did indeed go to Elberon on the Jersey Shore in July, de rigueur for members of our crowd. I was unaware of this fact because when my grandfather died, my aunt Marion whisked my grandmother off to a rented, rather rambling shingled house in East Hampton. On Lily Pond Lane no less. Aunt Marion did not marry a member of our crowd but a certain George Carhart, a man who existed in a world as far from the one occupied by that crowd as could possibly be imagined. Their life together consisted of sitting on the same banquette at El Morocco sipping champagne night after night. That apple certainly fell very far from my tree.

Mrs. George Carhart née Beer aside, I thoroughly enjoyed my life outside the crowd. Still, I was missing something, and I'm not referring to the religious ritual and traditions—although none of my Jewish friends had any instruction or training themselves. Virtually none. Still, it would have added another dimension to my life. At least they enjoyed certain Jewish traditions along with some obvious perks. I might have enjoyed romping with Randy Guggenheim and Ralph and Pam Colin, the future Lady Harlech, at The Century Country Club in Purchase, and I would have been interested to taste their famously fabulous food. The members there might have paid more attention to me had they known that on June 11, 1925, my grandfather was honored for his service on behalf of that Century Country Club. He was retiring as treasurer and a letter of appreciation was signed by Messrs. Schiff, Walburg, Sulzberger, Seligman, and Rothschild, of the Brooklyn branch, and many others.

At eighty-seven, at last I'm beginning to think about my Jewish heritage and tentatively take some pride in it. I go each summer to our family's country retreat in Keene Valley in the Adirondacks to stay at the Ausable Club, where at the Saturday-night buffet those members who line up for cold lobsters are most definitely not part of our crowd. Next summer, I want to take my children to see Knollwood on Lower Saranac, where my father stayed in one of the six birch-bark-framed cottages—Sulzbergers and Nathans on one side, the Marshalls and Blumenthals on the other. I would like to show them the casino where everyone, dressed formally, took their meals, since the cottages did not have proper kitchens in the early days. I would show them the wood-paneled boathouse down by the lake where you could hear the gentle waves lap against Mrs. Blumenthal's ancient highly polished wood boat parked at the dock. I want them to see this so fondly remembered place.

Aunt Elsie's property in Dobbs Ferry was divided into fourteen lots from which the distant view of the Hudson is now

The Century Country Club
Purchase, N. Y.

...esentation to Walter E. Beer
...June 11, 1925 — in appreciation
...r his many years of service in
...behalf of the Century Country Club.

*Walter E. Beer is honored by
The Century Country Club.*

obscured by a cluster of tract houses. Of course, no thought was given to keeping some of the magnificent copper beeches. As for those proper leisurely Sunday lunches at Aunt Alice's summer place in Hartsdale, I doubt if the ladies still sit in black-and-

Knollwood on Lower Saranac Lake.
My father's family had one of the six,
almost identical, cottages there.

The Ausable Club, St. Huberts, New York. Hope Colt on
the club's porch. Her family first came to the valley in 1873.

white-printed dresses and are served by an Irish maid, also
dressed in white, or that anyone wears white on the tennis court,
if it still exists. It all seems unlikely in the age of handheld devices
and religiously watched afternoon football games. It is sometimes hard for me to believe that the world I only half remember
ever existed. But it did in those seemingly simple but utterly gracious country places.

LUNCHING AT
LA TOUR D'ARGENT

THE DAY OF THE NOTRE DAME FIRE, APRIL 15, 2019, and much of the next I spent fighting back tears, mostly unsuccessfully. Soon after, I felt a little better; the great cathedral was saved. This was a miracle considering the fact that authorities said that if the inferno had gone on for another twenty minutes the fabled historic symbol of Paris would have been reduced to a smoldering pile of rubble, unimaginable to anyone who has spent more than a few hours in that magical city, which had so impressed me when I first visited in 1951.

As an architect, I have always been aware that Notre Dame's interior space is not quite as awe inspiring as that of a few other Gothic cathedrals built a bit later. The start of its construction followed closely after the cathedral of St. Denis, acknowledged to be the first built in the truly Gothic style with its fully devel-

......

My grandfather, father, John, and me. My ever-elegant grandfather wore spats, even in the West Village.

oped pointed arches and flying buttresses that support thin walls of masonry and the stained glass between.

In terms of height, Chartres and Reims are more visibly soaring, outdone only by the builders of the cathedral of Beauvais, whose creators' overreaching ambitions caused the nave to collapse. Notre Dame's stained-glass windows are not as famous as the incomparable ones at Chartres, although the rose windows at each end of the transept are as spectacular as any others and were mercifully saved. What does make Notre Dame special among cathedrals is the impression that it makes on the outside: It is monumental. On the west side, two triumphantly affirmative rectilinear towers, visible on the skyline from most of the city, exude strength and stability. On the east, the soaring flying buttresses rising above and reflecting in the Seine create a singularly strong impression. The spire and the roof are gone, but the views of the exterior, so loved now and throughout the centuries, remain. Truly a miracle.

One of the best, and certainly the most expensive, places to appreciate the view of those stalwart towers and flying buttresses is from perhaps the world's most famous restaurant, La Tour d'Argent. I do not frequent three-starred restaurants in Paris, partly for financial reasons, but also because their illustrious chefs are so seemingly obsessed with maintaining their hard-earned stars that they produce minuscule mystery concoctions without a trace of the much-maligned rich haute cuisine sauces I crave. La Tour d'Argent has lost all but one of its stars and, as I remember, it has less pretentious food, maybe

Notre Dame Cathedral,
Paris. Thank goodness
all the rose windows
were spared in the
2019 fire.

La Tour D'Argent, Paris. I have fought hard for one of those prized window tables.

even serving a quenelle or two along with the famous pressed duck, which I have yet to taste.

I assume that those ducks were served when my grandfather

Walter Beer dined with Eugene Meyer, the financier and future owner of *The Washington Post* and father of its publisher Kay Graham. Before World War I they dined together so often that a dish they fancied was named Eggs Meyerbeer after them, and apparently not after the composer of the long, elaborate, French grand operas. This piece of family history was relayed to me by my famously honest father, and my recollection of this strikingly handsome, eminently elegant, spats-wearing gentleman, my grandfather, allows me to believe this tale might be true. Family history aside, lunching at La Tour d'Argent is about more than the food and the elegantly cheerful sun-drenched interior. For me and the others vying for a window-side table, we are there for that view of flying buttresses and towers—magnificent and awe inspiring whether seen from the street or from the sixth-floor restaurant. And thanks to a miracle, the view remains magnificent for now and for future generations. Thank God.

"NO McDONALD'S ON 66"

RUMMAGING AROUND IN THE STORAGE AREA OF his Connecticut house, my son, Andrew, discovered a relic of what is by now the distant past. It was a square black placard on a wooden stick with white letters that read NO MCDONALD'S ON 66. Once delivered to my apartment, it brought back memories of a long-forgotten community battle fought in 1974. That year, in fact, was the one in which Nixon resigned. At the time, this protest created quite a stir. In two days sitting behind two card tables placed on the sidewalks of Lexington and Madison avenues, my wife Meme, our children Elizabeth and Andrew, our longtime loyal housekeeper Julia Gafney, and a friend

......

NO MCDONALD'S ON 66 placard overlaid on the distinguished façade of our landmarked building. Such signs were used to rally the troops to defeat McDonald's citywide expansion.

obtained sixteen thousand signatures demanding that McDonald's refrain from building a stand-alone one-story structure on
the corner of 66th Street and Lexington Avenue. This contro-

Meme and Elizabeth, wearing white, relaxing in our two-story living room. Part of a series of family photographs taken by noted American photographer Toni Frissell.

The living room at 131 East 66th Street.
Not to be outdone, the kitties wore white, too.

versy was not settled until the very day Nixon left Washington by helicopter, August 9 of that year.

Fewer than three months earlier, on Memorial Day weekend, my family and I were ensconced in our apartment on two floors of a Platt-and-Platt-designed, landmarked building on the northeast corner of 66th and Lexington. We were not in Bridgehampton, the Hudson Valley, or the northwest corner of Connecticut. Unlike our neighbors, we were spending the weekend in town. It was a hot, humid Saturday morning, and I happened to be looking out my library window when I saw quite a lot of activity in front of the Abbey Funeral Home directly across the avenue from me. I went downstairs, though actually I summoned the oh-so-quaint manually operated back elevator to slowly lower me to the lobby. Once there, I asked the doorman Tommy what was causing the commotion shattering the calm of my deserted neighborhood. He told me that the funeral home was being torn down to make way for a McDonald's.

Some might have been enamored with the thought of devouring quarter-pound Big Macs so conveniently, but I most assuredly was not. In fact, I was appalled at the idea of a fast-food emporium replete with gabled roof crowned by a blazing-yellow M-embossed sign interrupting my view of the Whitney stable, the deco Cosmopolitan Club, and the massive, brick-clad Armory, all, incidentally, landmarked. It would have been a most unhappy juxtaposition of the timeworn and the decidedly trashy. My neighbors echoed my indignation when they re-

Edward L Koch campaigned in our neighborhood when he ran briefly for mayor in 1973. We gave three fundraisers in our living room when he did run and win in 1977.

turned from their leafy retreats and were informed of this im-pending intrusion. I will not detail all of the many machinations involved in furthering our fight, but I will list a few.

The first step was to inform our Community Planning Board 8 and their leader Edith Fisher, who could not have been more helpful. As it happened, there was at the time a heated mayoral contest involving Carter Burden and Ed Koch, who both found it convenient to gain support by appearing at board meetings and speaking to our neighbors from a raised platform in front of the stained-glass window in our two-story living room. McDonald's appeared to have no idea of the neighbor-hood where they were planning to plant their franchise or they would have avoided tearing down the innocuous four-story building that housed those funerals and substituting hamburgers and french fries for corpses and coffins. Forthwith, we informed them on whose toes they were treading, starting most conspicuously with David Rockefeller, whose sprawling red-brick town house was a mere two blocks away. In a book describing this campaign, *McDonald's: Behind the Arches,* Mr. Rockefeller infers that he was influential in our movement and, in so doing, evoked the wrath of the men in Oak Brook, Illinois, by threatening to withdraw their money from Chase Manhattan. This may be true, but he was never personally involved with our campaign. The people who lent their well-known names were Peggy Rockefeller not David, Blanchette Rockefeller not John, Betsey Whitney not Jock, Iphigene Sulzberger not her son Arthur. All those famous-named women belonged to the Cosmopolitan Club and along with many other members provided much-appreciated support. This may not have been all that surprising, for it is difficult picturing Peggy Rockefeller traipsing up Lexington Avenue to place two orders of burgers, fries, and giant Cokes on a Thursday evening, maid's night out, then serving David on a tray in front of the TV in their library upstairs.

It helped that the Church of St. Vincent Ferrer, another landmarked building on that corner, and the Park East Synagogue around the corner provided a plethora of priests, nuns, and rabbis for our near-nightly rallies in front of our deserted site, also covered conscientiously by channels 2, 4, 7, and 11 on the six o'clock news. The *Times* wrote three editorials in support, *New York* Magazine ran a cover story by Mimi Sheraton, and I swallowed two Valiums in order to appear on the then popular Arthur Godfrey show, whose host was completely baffled as to why he was interviewing me. I fear we gathered few supporters in the hinterlands, but their voices were never needed. Indeed, not only did we stop McDonald's from building their outlet across from me, but the fight discouraged them from opening similar stores every ten blocks, all the way up Lexington Avenue.

The McDonald's campaign involved a fight to save our hearth and home from suffering a foreign object invading our very privileged enclave. Happily, other protests were inspired

The Cosmopolitan Club. This landmarked club on East 66th Street had many socially conscious members.

by less parochial concerns. On May 3, 1963, when President
Kennedy was in office, fellow architects Max Bond, his wife
Jean, Meme, and I, boarded the Metroliner bound for Wash-
ington to stage a four-person protest in front of the White

*The family marching in Central Park. Many protests happened
there and in Washington, DC, against the war in Iraq, against
banning abortions, and for more AIDS research.*

House expressing our outrage at the use of snapping attack dogs against the demonstrators in Birmingham. As it happened, on the taxi ride from Union Station traveling along Pennsylvania Avenue, we heard that the dispute had been settled. Abandoning our neatly lettered placards, we accepted Jacqueline Kennedy's broadcasted invitation to tour the White House. Soon after, those discarded placards were replaced with ones declaring that there should be no war in Iraq and that women most definitely had the right to choose.

Inevitably, our familial social activism became focused on the AIDS epidemic once the extent of its devastation became known. I started distributing food and groceries at St. Peter's Church until I turned to fundraising benefits—three of which involved a cabaret Upstairs at The Russian Tea Room, generously given by the talented and glamorous Yana Avis.

After all that time, one placard with white letters on a black background was not discarded and is now in the dusty bin in my current apartment located farther up Lexington from a former site of our campaign. There it will stay until I am gone, the apartment sold, the bin emptied, and the placard thrown out onto the sidewalk where incurious strangers will not know or care why in 1974 it seemed so important to gather on sweltering summer evenings and raise placards declaring NO MCDONALD'S ON 66.

BMOC

"ARE YOU IN, SHORT BEER?" THERE WAS AN AUTHORI-
tarian quality to the voice, an insistence, that told me that the
speaker was not one of my freshman classmates at Phillips Exeter Academy. My room was in Dunbar Hall, which was re-
served for the first-year students, and although some of my
classmates had not quite reached full growth, I was in a class by
myself in the diminutive stature department, reaching only four
feet nine inches in height. I had already earned the name Short
Beer, not to be derisive, but to differentiate myself from my
older brother John Beer, already in his junior year, an upper-
middler. The question as to why these lofty giants were seeking
me out was soon answered. "How would you like to play a
body?" "A body?" I asked in a somewhat shaky soprano voice.
One of the circling giants explained that the Dramatic Association was putting on a play, *Arsenic and Old Lace,* which required a
body to be hidden in an onstage window seat and later carried

......

Phillips Exeter Academy Dramatic Association productions in 1949.
That fetching manicurist in Boy Meets Girl *(top left) is me.*

offstage. My very existence raised the possibility that such a task would be less than arduous. I agreed to be their body.

Three years passed and I was elected president of the Dramatic Association, having designed the sets for all the subsequent school plays. I could, with a little makeup and an appropriate wig, pass as a rather fetching female. This transformation made me much in demand. At that time Exeter still did not admit girls, and as a result boys played the girls' parts. I was a medieval maiden in Shakespeare's *Henry IV, Part 1,* a patriot's wife in Shaw's *The Devil's Disciple,* and a cheeky manicurist in Bella and Samuel Spewack's *Boy Meets Girl.* Along with that, for reasons unknown, one evening I entered the school gymnasium and joined in an unscripted tableau vivant astride two seniors making like an elephant, which I straddled wearing a glittering gown replete with a bare midriff crowned by a flowing feather headdress. My appearance inspired thunderous applause, no jeering in evidence, not even from the very large southern contingent or from the few Buckley boys who had transferred from that rather straitlaced school in New York. Despite my occasional flamboyant appearances, I was considered a wheel, a big man on campus, a BMOC.

In the 1950s much was being written about boys who were somewhat different being bullied by classmates and teachers alike. John Knowles's *A Separate Peace* and Robert Anderson's play *Tea and Sympathy* explored this theme. Both authors, incidentally, went to Exeter. Seeing the play soon after graduation, I was suitably moved by Deborah Kerr's words as she fingered her blouse and said suggestively, "Years from now when you talk about this, and you will, be kind." No master's wife sacrificed her honor for me, as I never needed saving.

It was the year 1948 that saw me transformed into a body. That was also the year the first Negro, as Blacks were called then, was admitted into a private boarding school. His name was Monroe Dowling, later Dr. Dowling. Since Monty lived in a different dorm from mine and had different interests, I did not know him well. He was immediately elected president of the freshman class, perhaps an overreaction to his somewhat conspicuous arrival in our midst. From seeing him at various reunions in the following years, I gather his time at the school was not without struggles. As my classmate John Pope told me, "I think being a Black kid sent off to a school with 750 white teenage boys in 1948 must have been as close to hell as anything I can imagine." Mercifully, my experience was different. Because our class contained boys from forty-seven of the then forty-eight states, we all in our individual ways were different. Even so, I credit the masters at Exeter for fostering a climate of tolerance. As such, my skirts and my wigs were not cause for derision, and for a couple of years I was allowed to feel that I was a BMOC.

HAPPY, HAPPY, HAPPY

I T WAS A HOT, HUMID DAY IN SHANGHAI. I TOOK LITTLE notice as I perused the new Armani store before taking an elevator to the fifth floor in the same building, Three on the Bund, to be exact. My destination was the restaurant Jean-Georges, also recently opened. Upon arrival, I passed by a dramatic seven-story interior atrium designed by my Harvard Graduate School of Design classmate Michael Graves on my way to a window table that looked out on the newly built skyscrapers across the highly trafficked Huangpu River. It was August 2001.

I look back on these steamy summer days with great pleasure. The city's extraordinary renaissance was still in its formative stage. That Armani outlet was the first international high-fashion store to open; there may be as many as twenty Armani stores now, rivaled by still more Chanels. To me, Shanghai

......

The Peninsula Shanghai. Top: The rooftop bar, Sir Elly's Terrace, looking toward Pudong. Bottom: Tyree relaxes in the hotel's garden, which formerly belonged to the English Consulate.

exuded the freshness of spring's first blossoming. Although I was thoroughly enjoying myself that first summer, I was not in town on a lark-like holiday. I had been asked by the Hong Kong and Shanghai Hotels Ltd., and its chairman, the Honorable Sir Michael Kadoorie, to enter an international competition for the design of an apartment, shopping, and parking complex to

The Bund, Shanghai. The Peninsula hotel (far right) anchors the group of historic buildings to the south. Also bordering the garden, the former English Consulate residence.

include, first and foremost, a 260-room Peninsula hotel on the only remaining underdeveloped site on the historic, broad riverside thoroughfare, the Bund. My initial enthusiastic response to the city must have inspired me. I won the competition.

As the scheme further developed, it was determined that this oversized project should harmonize with and enhance the

existing row of historic landmarked buildings, many neoclassical, others decidedly deco, all in their way interesting. Such diversity creates a remarkably harmonious whole. The Peninsula site is at the very north end, the last major one on the Bund. Some architects would use this as an excuse to make a dramatic individual statement, a monument to their own originality and towering talent, treating the rest of the Bund's complex of buildings as a mere background to the architect's virtuosity. I took a different tack, which eventually afforded me one of the most satisfying moments of my professional life.

The last phase on this job I spent in Hong Kong, interacting directly with the clients in their offices, and so I had not seen the near-finished building for almost a year. Finally in Shanghai again, I decided to first view the complex from afar, on the terrace of the restaurant M on the Bund, a venerable establishment by Shanghai standards that had opened ten years before.

Fortified with a glass of Sancerre in hand, I gazed north. For quite a long moment, I could not discern the hotel, so well did it blend with the existing historic buildings. I thought, *Good job, David!*

The Peninsula has by now been joined by several other five-star hotels. New office buildings are everywhere, replacing charming low brick structures that had been clustered around narrow alleys and courtyards. Many towers have been built in the historic French Concession, although their intrusive bulk and height is largely concealed by branches of thousands of large leafy linden trees originally planted by the French. They arch over avenues and streets alike, defusing the view of those offending towers.

It's still very pleasant walking the narrow streets of the Concession to Sasha's, a simple restaurant in the two-story building once home to the then young Soong sisters. As you walk through to the somewhat scruffy but nevertheless pleasant backyard, you pass by a portrait of all three—one who famously married for money, one who married for love of her country, and one who married for power, Madame Chiang Kai-shek. Nearby is Sun Yat-sen's house, amazing in its simplicity considering that he was modern China's first president. Farther on, traveling down twisting streets, you might lunch on a veranda in the secluded garden of the English Consulate General, now the restaurant Yongfoo Elite.

In an audacious display of Chinese ingenuity, the existing neoclassical opera house was moved, intact, thirty yards to make way for a new highway. That did not dissuade the city from building a new, much larger one aptly named the Shanghai Grand Theatre. In this vast, handsome auditorium I heard Wagner's complete *Ring* cycle performed for the first time in

The French Concession, Shanghai. A shaded street (top) and Sasha's restaurant (bottom), the former home of the Soong sisters.

the city by the Cologne Opera before a rapt audience of mostly
young locals. On virtually every trip, I have managed to visit the
superb Shanghai Museum if only to see the magnificent ancient
bronzes, which alone justify a fifteen-hour flight from JFK.

My newly late husband, Tyree Giroux, was more than a little

*The Peninsula Shanghai. All-day dining in the lobby, definitely not a
coffee shop. The interior designer was Pierre-Yves Rochon.*

obsessive about returning to China, and we had planned a trip for early May. He succumbed to the coronavirus in early April 2020, and I am apprehensive about taking any trips without him since ours together were so magical. When it's possible I will travel again to Shanghai, lunch under the trees in the gar-

dens of the French Concession, stroll along the Bund, and spend my nights at the Peninsula. While there, I will appreciate even more the grand but humanely scaled lobby that looks out onto the lush tree-lined garden once enjoyed by the British Consulate General. I will dine in the other two restaurants, but what I am looking forward to most is taking the elevator to the top, to the rooftop outdoor bar, Sir Elly's Terrace, where I'll again enjoy the absolutely spectacular view. To the right you can see the artfully illuminated collection of historic buildings that line the Bund; to the left across the river the dramatic skyline now boasts even taller skyscrapers, many of which sport loony leaping lights. To say the least, breathtaking. I am happy that I had a chance to design this hotel. I am happy that it involved visiting this magical city so often. Most of all, I am happy to have shared it with my dear, sweet Tyree.

GRAND HOTEL

THE BEER FAMILY DID NOT TAKE CORONATION YEAR 1953 lightly. My parents planned a family trip to the British Isles that summer, even scheduling to be in Edinburgh at the time of Princess Elizabeth's crowning. Once there, we cheered Her Majesty on the street in front of St. Giles'. We had crossed the Atlantic on the *Queen Elizabeth* in medium grandeur, in cabin class, not first, of course. I say "of course" because that booking characterized our family's lifestyle. Although we lived on Park Avenue, it was in an undistinguished red-brick rental building, untouched by the genius of architecture Rosario Candela, the designer of the avenue's finest apartment houses. We summered not in Southampton, but in Keene Valley far north in the far-from-fancy part of the Adirondacks. My mother did not lunch

......

The newly created Astor Court and King Cole Bar at The St. Regis New York. The two-story space was once a small storeroom.

The King Cole Bar. After all these years, it is nice to still be recognized by the bartenders.

at La Côte Basque but more often at Gino's, surrounded by those leaping zebras that pranced all over the walls. She shopped at Bloomingdales and B. Altman, not Bergdorf's, and when my parents traveled to London, they stayed at Brown's not Claridge's. Why, then, did I become so enamored with the lore and legacy of grand hotels? When I traveled alone to Greece in 1955, I stayed in the simplest hotels imaginable, ones down dark alleys and with no elevators. That said, I did spend a considerable number of hours haunting the halls of one hotel in Athens that could be called grand, the venerable Grande Bretagne. In the old days, before it was modernized and saddled with endless billowing satin and silk curtains and cushions, the hotel had a sparse, slightly mysterious "best of the Balkans" feel to it. No doubt Agatha Christie stayed there in order to break her three-day trip on the *Orient Express* from Dover to Istanbul, of course staying at the legendary Pera Palace Hotel there. Although I never slept in a room at the GB, as it is known to this day, I spent considerable time in the original dark and musty bar overhearing A. C. Sedgwick, the *New York Times* correspondent, pontificating on world events.

Years later, when in London, Paris, and Rome, I was less interested in sparse authenticity than in out-and-out luxury. While sipping a glass of white wine in one of the elegantly appointed bars of The Connaught in London, Le Bristol Paris, or Le Grand Hotel in Rome, I would put the glass aside and sneak upstairs to check out the guest rooms where the maids had left the doors open while cleaning. Such surreptitious tours became more enjoyable when I could afford to lunch at the magnificent Ritz Restaurant in London and the deco-inspired Relais Plaza in Paris, or enjoy a crustless club sandwich with extra chips in the spectacular high-domed lobby of Rome's Le Grand Hotel.

Those years of indulgent but serious surveying were put to

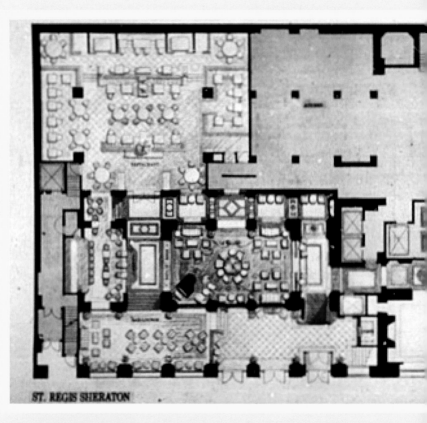

ST. REGIS SHERATON

The St. Regis New York. My preliminary first sketch. All the ground-floor spaces reconfigured and, except for the front desk area, redesigned. The newly placed King Cole Bar (far left) was finally enlarged considerably and can now be seen from the front desk area.

good use when in 1981 Sheraton entrusted the renovation of The St. Regis New York to our newly formed firms Brennan Beer Gorman / Architects and Brennan Beer Gorman Monk / Interiors. In New York, many deluxe hotels had been closed or torn down—the Ritz-Carlton Hotel on Madison Avenue as

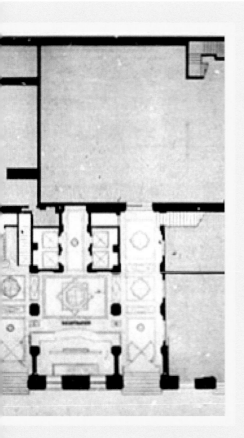

well as the Astor and the Knickerbocker in Times Square. The Plaza was certainly grand, but very large with many substandard rooms—just like the Waldorf Astoria. The Peninsula, formerly the Gotham Hotel, had suffered an unfortunate renovation by Pierre Cardin who attempted to turn the hotel into Maxim's of Paris, which he owned at the time. Finally, the St. Regis was a neglected wreck also having many tiny rooms. The original grand lobby on Fifth Avenue was replaced by several revenue-producing stores. The famous King Cole Bar was placed obscurely at the back of the hotel in a nightclub setting for the famous Maxfield Parrish mural.

Our firm decided to demolish the interior of the entire

778 Park Avenue

November 8, 1990

Dear Mr. Tischmann:

This is a very belated thank you for the wonderful visit I had at the St. Regis. I kept thinking of Vincent and of how very proud he would be to see the hotel coming back even more beautiful than it was when his father built it. It was really a very moving experience for me and I appreciate your taking up so very much of your time to show it to me and to have given me such a memorable visit.

Marietta Tree has asked me to say something at the opening and I am delighted to do it.

Most Sincerely

Brooke Astor.

cc: David Beer

Mrs. Vincent Astor's letter thanking the St. Regis for the tour I gave her. At least she copied me.

hotel including all the guest room floors except for the first-floor check-in area and the smallish ballroom on the second floor, the Versailles Room. All of the guest rooms were reconfigured to be equally spacious, with newly designed bathrooms featuring a stall shower as well as a bathtub and two sinks. On the ground floor several 55th Street stores were eliminated and a new two-story gathering place, the Astor Court, was created. The newly placed King Cole Bar was moved and made visible from the front desk. My brilliant interior design partner Gustin Tan and I spent Saturday mornings in the period Wrightsman Rooms at the Metropolitan Museum measuring the height of chair moldings from the floor. The hotel was never to be a pastiche of eighteenth-century French architecture. In terms of those details, we created the real thing.

Back then I had a special feeling for the rooftop ballroom, the St. Regis Roof. I had been invited to several family parties there in my youth and appreciated its intimate festive feeling. In fact, I was second escort at my great friend Susannah Ryan's coming-out party there. My duty was to toast her parents, which I did after calming my nerves with two glasses of champagne. Not surprisingly, I strongly expressed my affection for the Roof when Sheraton, over my objections, decided to demolish the rooftop ballroom and turn the space into luxury suites. As it happened, I was asked to be a last-minute guest at a dinner being given that very evening by my esteemed eye doctor Dr. John Espy and his wife, Polly. Once seated I asked my dinner partner her name, which as usual I didn't bother to learn. My unknown table mate asked me what I was doing and I quite quickly answered that I was redesigning the St. Regis, a job that thrilled me, except for the fact that the Roof was to be demolished. The effect of my news upon her was instantaneous. Without further ado, she asked a waiter where she could find a phone, stood up, and was gone. The next day I learned the reason for her abrupt departure. The phone-seeking lady was Jessie Araskog, wife of Rand Araskog, the chairman of ITT and the Sheraton Corporation, and she had called the president of Sheraton. The Roof was saved.

Just before the formal reopening it was my duty and distinct pleasure to show Brooke Astor around the almost finished hotel. She had lived there with her husband, Vincent Astor, for several years in the 1950s. At the end of the tour, she raised her gloved hand and said, "Why, it's just as I remember from when Vincent and I lived here." Thanking her, I did not add that it was, in fact, virtually all new. For Mrs. Astor, and fortunately many New Yorkers, the St. Regis was reborn once more a Grand Hotel.

The St. Regis Roof. It was saved by a dinner party.

THE
OLD HOUSE

“JUST WAIT UNTIL YOU HEAR THE FINAL TRIO,” MY great-uncle Arthur Harlow said to me during the last intermission of Gounod's *Faust,* which was being performed at the New York City Center. I suppose he was encouraging me to stay the course, although I had no intention of leaving. And yes, at the end I was suitably impressed by Faust's entreating, Mephistopheles's gloating, and Marguerite's exulting as she ascended miraculously to heaven. This first operatic experience occurred when I had just turned seven.

I have no recollection where we were sitting for that first *Faust,* although my uncle Arthur was not the sort of man who would suffer inferior seats. Neither would those who later treated me to a seat at many operatic performances at the old Met on 39th Street. And what a seat it was! On even Monday

The Metropolitan Opera House in 1966. Inset, top: Maria Callas debuts in Norma on October 29, 1956. Inset, bottom: I am exuding pride in front of the New House.

nights the Irving Berlin family—including my chum, the youngest daughter Elizabeth—enjoyed a just-off-center box where
Mrs. Berlin's stepmother, the legendary soprano Anna Case,
sat. Aunt Anna, as she was referred to by all the children, was
famous for two things. She was the first to play Sophie in the
American premiere of *Der Rosenkavalier* under Toscanini, and
on these evenings she always wore a necklace that held the
Mackay Emerald enthroned on her more-than-ample bosom.
Though that emerald was reputed to be the largest in the world,
the eldest Berlin sister, Mary Ellen Barrett, rather irreverently
referred to it as a guest-sized piece of Palmolive soap. Even so,
it shone so brilliantly that at times it was difficult to say which
was more dazzling, the jewel shining from the lights on the
stage or the illustrious singers who performed during those
golden years—Milanov and Tebaldi, Stevens and Thebom,
Tucker and Björling, Merrill and Warren. Golden indeed.

For some reason, the moment I remember best occurred
after I had returned from the in-house restaurant Sherry's and
was sitting in my seat, appropriately dressed in my father's ancient Brooks Brothers tailcoat and surrounded by that caring
family. When that wonderful orchestra started playing the stir-
ring strains of the third-act overture of *Lohengrin*, and I listened
to the music swell up in front of the famous golden curtain, I
felt for a moment the luckiest man on earth.

By my late teens, my interest in opera had grown greatly.
One summer while studying architecture at the École des
Beaux-Arts at Fontainebleau just outside Paris, I suddenly de-

The old Metropolitan Opera House opened on October 22, 1888. Its gold curtain shone on Tebaldi, Price, Horne, and Sutherland.

cided to take a three-day on-and-off third-class train trip to Bayreuth to hear Birgit Nilsson and Wolfgang Windgassen sing in *Tristan and Isolde*. The fact that I was embarking on this arduous journey without first securing a ticket didn't faze me. My optimism was duly rewarded as I secured the first turned-in ticket, allowing me to sit in one of those famously uncomfortable wooden seats in the Festspielhaus. Even my aching backside did not keep me from taking serious snoozes, although fortunately I was thoroughly awake for the climactic "Liebestod."

*The Metropolitan Opera Club in the New House
is a gracious place to enjoy dinner while attending
a performance.*

In a similar vein in 1956, two classmates and I from the Harvard Graduate School of Design came down from Cambridge and waited in line twenty-four hours for standing-room tickets for Maria Callas's opening in *Norma* at the Met. Brandishing slide rules, we sat on the sidewalk studying for our exams, passing the hours fruitfully. It was at that performance that I proved that horses are not the only creatures that can sleep standing up, but at least I was awake for her sensational "Casta Diva."

Another fortuitous time in the Old House involved the aftermath of a super-serious snowstorm on January 27, 1961. My adventure started in the Plaza's Grand Ballroom, where I had been persuaded at the very last minute by a friend to attend a party with the unpromising name of The American Library in Paris Ball, apparently chaired by a certain Laura Houghton—Meme to her friends. She was absolutely gorgeous in a pink-and-white-striped Balmain ball dress. Superficial to the core, I cut in for several dances that evening. She gave at least some indication that she was not entirely displeased. A few days later, after that enormous blizzard, I was inspired to pick up the phone and ask Meme if she would like to trudge with me through the snowdrifts down to the Old House to hear Leontyne Price and Franco Corelli make their Metropolitan Opera broadcast debut in *Trovatore.* I told her that I did not have tickets, but that we were pretty certain to get standing-room tickets because of the severity of the storm the night before. I thought that this might be a welcome change of pace for her since she had spent the last couple of years very comfortably ensconced in the American embassy residence in Paris during her father's time as American ambassador to France. She agreed. We secured our standing-room tickets and stood dutifully behind the barrier until the rather jaunty overture started. I spied two empty seats in the front row. We moved there somewhat surreptitiously and were suitably thrilled by the performance.

We were married early the following year before eight hundred people in Christ Church, Corning, New York.

The New House opened in the fall of 1966 at Lincoln Center. John Canaday of *The New York Times* called it "retardatory avant-gardism," and Ada Louise Huxtable scorned it as a "throwback." Its maybe-modern interior has, through the years, become rather dear to me, right up to the ridiculous Frito-like artwork precariously perched atop the proscenium arch. Perhaps that curiosity is the secret of the hall's miraculous acoustics, allowing both trumpet-voiced Birgit Nilsson and soft-singing Judith Blegen to be heard in the top row of the balcony, the Family Circle.

Of course, I have done my share of grousing about the new productions. I was far from thrilled to find the two villa-owning sisters from Ferrara transformed into bobby-socks-wearing boobies from Brooklyn in *Così Fan Tutte,* or Maria Theresa lowering herself to associate with preening prostitutes before bidding adieu to her barely pubescent lover Octavian in *Der Rosenkavalier.* But two Philip Glass operas were performed with such dazzling ingenuity that even the minimalist-music haters were impressed. The somberly set *Dialogues of the Carmelites* is perfection and I hope will never be replaced. And I am always happy when Zeffirelli's spectacular and at the same time sensitive production of *La Bohème* survives yet another year, saved from destruction.

I have been a member of the Metropolitan Opera Club for over fifty years and attend the Met almost weekly. It has become one of the hallmarks of my life in New York. If I fancy a particular performance, I direct a taxi to cross the park to Lincoln Center as many as four times to hear it. Once inside, I cross the seriously congested lobby to take the club members' private elevator to the Club Room, which boasts an Angelo Donghia–designed silver-leafed ceiling lit by a circular crystal chandelier. After downing a hurriedly produced Sancerre, I proceed to one of the members' front-side boxes to attend what I hope will be another memorable performance at the Metropolitan Opera House.

Now, in March 2021, I am about to flee the frigid winds that freeze my fingers as I walk along Lexington Avenue and spend a month in Palm Beach sequestered in a single room in a fairly small hotel with my iPhone, not my old portable radio, to my ear, listening to previously recorded matinee performances that will bring back memories of the days when Tebaldi, Tucker, and Warren sang so thrillingly in that fondly remembered, never-to-be-forgotten Old House.

SAVING VENICE

IN THE 1940S, BEFORE GOING AWAY TO BOARDING
school, I spent many Saturday afternoons lunching with my
parents at a corner table in the cozy low-ceilinged bar/restau-
rant in The Sherry-Netherland on 59th and Fifth. In those
postwar years, going out for Saturday lunch was still quite de
rigueur. My parents' friends, the ones who were seemingly sat-
isfied with their comparatively simple lives, opted to lunch at
Pierre's, a reasonably priced French bistro on East 53rd Street
soon to be demolished to make way for Lever House. Their
conspicuously more well-heeled friends retired to a front banquette in the hushed elegance of either La Caravelle or La Gre-
nouille, both nearby. Going their own way, Florence and Walter
Beer chose their usual Fifth Avenue location. Almost before
our winter coats were whisked away, my parents put in their
order for two martinis made with gin, not vodka, and eggs
Benedict made not with ham but with omega-3-infused smoked

....

*Inset, top: In the garden of the Hotel Cipriani, Venice. Lunch with hats
while Saving Venice. Inset, bottom: Larry Lovett's terrace on the Grand
Canal, where all the visiting dignitaries were entertained.*

salmon. Worth noting, in those days, no one sanctimoniously said, "I never drink at lunch," as they do almost universally today. Killjoys!

It was about those fondly remembered days with my parents that I was thinking a couple of years ago when I walked into the same conspicuously low-ceilinged space in The Sherry-Netherland now occupied by the rather grand, decidedly un-trattoria-like restaurant Arrigo Cipriani. It had been almost twenty years since I was there, but when I saw the low ceiling and low tables covered with off-white tablecloths, I immediately thought of another low-ceilinged restaurant I had once known so well, Harry's Bar in Venice. It was a Proustian experience remembering lunching there, eating a risotto primavera accompanied by a bubbling Bellini. I was usually sitting with friends gossiping away happily about what we had heard and seen at one of the very special events planned for our enjoyment by board members Larry Lovett, Bob Guthrie, and Director Beatrice Guthrie of Save Venice, a charity dedicated to the preservation of Venice's endangered works of arts and monuments. On several first September Sundays, assorted types from Europe and America came to town, Vuitton-wheeling: a general mixture of rather-royals including Prince and Princess Michael of Kent, and Princess Marianne Sayn-Wittgenstein-Sayn from Salzburg; philanthropists Jayne Wrightsman and Deeda Blair; fashion designers Valentino, Givenchy, and Oscar de la Renta; socialites Nan Kempner and Lee Thaw; historian John Julius Norwich; and archaeologist Iris Love. Even Ivana Trump came, always traveling alone with her bodyguard, too grand for the likes of ordinary folks such as me. I rubbed their well-dressed shoulders with the rest on four separate Septembers, which is why I happened to be considered a regular at Harry's

Harry's Bar, Venice. Downstairs is the only place to be, served by Mirko.

Bar, always to be greeted effusively at the entrance by its ever-smiling owner Arrigo Cipriani.

On the morning of August 31, 1997, Arrigo most definitely was not smiling. With great solemnity, he told me that Princess Diana had died tragically in an automobile accident in Paris the night before. For one week, the chattering at Harry's Bar stopped. I am not sure whether we continued with the planned programs, since I spent most of my time watching CNN on my

*Left: Cipriani
Garden.
Nan Kemper
and Georgie
Abreu. Nan's
hat was the
largest.*

*Right: Sir John
Julius Norwich
and Iris Love,
concentrating while
on a Save Venice
excursion to Greece
and Turkey.*

extremely small television in my extremely large room at The
Gritti Palace hotel. A sense of sorrow prevailed. It was not until
the following September that the chattering and preening re-
sumed at Harry's Bar.

The Save Venice organization made our visits truly extraordinary. Even in the 1990s visiting the Basilica di San Marco was
a hassle, being jostled by tourists pointing their Instamatics to-

ward the soaring, glittering, mosaic-covered domes. We were
tourists, too, but when we visited the Basilica it was closed to
the public, as were the cloistered gardens of San Giorgio Mag-
giore, so we could lunch in peace after inspecting the interior of

Lee Thaw. Always Best Dressed, even when regarding a ruin.

Palladio's greatest early church. If at that time you happened to
be staying at Venice's most expensive and exclusive hotel, the
Cipriani, and wanted to stroll through their lushly planted gardens that border on the lagoon, you were out of luck: Our
groups of white-pant-sporting men and broad-rimmed straw-

The Villa Barbaro—also known as the Villa di Maser—
in Maser, Italy. Veronese's frescoes were given short shrift
by the Save Venice lunch bunch.

hat-wearing ladies had taken over the place for a delicious, sit-down lunch. On that day the cypress trees had never seemed so green, the lagoon so sparkling, so blue.

On one occasion, we traveled on buses to visit the Veneto and the Palladian Villa di Maser. Inside that charming edifice I suddenly found myself in a room admiring statuesque muses painted by Veronese and realized I was appreciating the frescoes in solitary splendor. The other art lovers had dashed to the garden to secure the best possible tables occupied by the most prestigious people. By the time I arrived, I was relegated to a far-off table sitting almost alone on the fringes of the garden, far from the center of things. It was then that I realized that proper placement, being *bien placé,* is considered more important than appreciating world-famous sixteenth-century Venetian frescoes by Veronese.

Art appreciation was not on the menu most evenings, which were spent in sumptuous private palaces that displayed even more paintings on the walls and frescoes on the ceilings, all lit by candles in glittering crystal chandeliers. At the end of these evenings, I found myself taking the last motorboat back to the Gritti. There I sipped a final glass of wine alone on the terrace, marveling at the stillness that had descended over the Grand Canal. A few remaining lights sparkled and all that was heard was an occasional cat crying, hoping to find some late-night company, and the soft lapping of tiny waves rippling along the edge of the dock.

ANOTHER DEATH
IN VENICE

WHILE THE CORONAVIRUS RAGED DURING THE
spring of 2020, my daughter insisted on a nearly complete
lockdown for me. No visitors, no family, no friends. She did
allow twice-weekly walks in Central Park with my trusty all-
knowing, all-healing physical therapist Sean Conroy, who en-
couraged me to walk ever faster, ever farther. Sean provided me
with one of his earbuds that supplied us with music as we
trudged through the park from my apartment on 90th Street
and Lexington Avenue to the terrace overlooking the sailboat
pond near 72nd Street.

One day I decided not to listen to that year's birthday boy,
Ludwig van Beethoven, opting for something a bit more challenging: a Mahler symphony, the Fifth to be exact. That particular selection was not all that challenging since the fourth

.....

Hotel Des Bains, Lido, Venice. On its terrace, Alexis Gregory holds court
with Sondra Gilman, Celso Gonzalez-Falla, and friend.

movement, the famous Adagietto, was familiar to me because the Italian director Luchino Visconti had used it so effectively in the 1971 film *Death in Venice,* based on Thomas Mann's novella. Sean, not unsurprisingly, suggested that under the current circumstances a piece involving a devastating plague was not what we most needed to hear as we strolled, socially distancing our way to the pond. Nevertheless I prevailed, and the Adagietto played softly in my ear for the rest of the afternoon's walk. It reminded me of the hotel in which Visconti's film was made, the Hotel Des Bains, located on Venice's Lido, across the lagoon from that celebrated city.

Walking along, I remembered the first time I stayed in Des Bains in 1951, when my aunt Ethel brought me and my cousin, future *Life* photographer and picture editor John Loengard, to Italy for a six-week visit. She was an inveterate traveler who believed in seeing one country really well, not several superficially. Having left from the Port of Newark, we began the trip in Genoa where we embarked after two weeks in a (very) slow freighter. We took in the monuments, frescoes, paintings, and statues in several Northern Italian cities, then arrived in Venice, well educated but somewhat satiated and near exhaustion. Happily, Aunt Ethel decided to take us to the seaside for a couple of days of relaxation. I fear all I remember of that visit was swimming in the Adriatic and more often in the hotel's swimming pool, reputed then to be the largest in Italy.

My memories of the hotel became more vivid through the years, as I stayed there quite frequently, sometimes with my

Hotel Des Bains. Top: Luciano Visconti filmed Death in Venice *here using period costumes in the beautifully restored dining room (bottom).*

daughter Elizabeth and my grandchildren, but more often alone. I would be picked up at the quay where the launches park and where the hotel's own mini buses would board the guests going to Des Bains. At first glimpse, you could see the hotel stretching along almost the entire length of the property facing

Hotel Des Bains. The swimming pool was reputed to be the largest hotel pool in Italy in 1951.

the sea with its symmetrical façade rising in the center to contain a large round clock placed over the entrance. A broad staircase, covered by a deep-red carpet, led to it. The hotel's most striking characteristic was the wide porch that extended to the far ends, uncovered except at the entrance. At the south end, the porch turned, allowing for outdoor dining overlooking the garden and pool. What I remember best about my early visits to that porch were the clinking coffee cups and tinkling glasses, enjoying the sound of the sea reaching the shore and the soft summer breezes rustling the Roman pines that surrounded that broad terrace.

The interior of the hotel had been lovingly restored for the film. The wood trim had been painted a crisp glossy white except for the dark mahogany used around a large two-story living room topped by an etched-glass ceiling. All the public rooms opened to that broad porch through tall French doors crowned by half-moon lunettes along the entire façade. Assorted potted palms and occasional arrangements of blue hydrangeas were the only embellishments. And oh yes, the wood floors creaked ever so slightly under scattered rugs in the lobby and runners on the long halls upstairs, which my grandchildren occasionally used for indoor competitive racing. Easy, breezy, a perfect setting for families to escape a Venetian summer's heat. Guests in distressed jeans, short shorts, and flip-flops never seemed completely out of place.

By contrast, families who stayed there at the turn of the century as pictured so vividly in the film comprised men in white ties and tails, women in narrow, straight long skirts and billowing, flower-covered hats, and young boys languidly lounging in crisp white sailor suits. Obviously this was not the attire worn by the Beer family when we visited. In deference to the hotel's fabled past, my jeans were not distressed and my shoes neither flipped nor flopped. On occasion—during the years I attended the Save Venice galas in that still, sultry first week of September—my look was a bit less casual. That week, we were extremely conscientious about sightseeing in the morning, going on guided trips to study the Tintorettos in the Scuola Grande di San Rocco and the two Titians in the Basilica dei Frari next door. But at lunchtime I was able to lure a few friends out to the Lido, perhaps for a swim and certainly for lunch under the yellow-and-white-striped awning. This was not a snack-by-the-pool kind of lunch. We started with Bellinis, then moved on to risotto primavera, followed by chilled poached salmon and white wine from the Veneto, all of it served by waiters wearing white jackets, black pants, and bow ties. For a brief moment the torn jeans and flip-flops were replaced by flowery frocks and broad straw hats on the women; on the men, linen shirts with colorful cashmere sweaters slung casually around their shoulders. Alexis and Georgie . . . Malcom and Yvetta . . . Gordon and Shelley . . . Ann and her handsome young son Paul . . . Marion and her lovely daughter Kate . . . and usually the irrepressible Principessa Ismene Chigi Della Rovere, known to many as the Downtown Princess because of her frequent visits to the likes of Area and Xenon. At some point CIGA, which

managed Des Bains, decided to downgrade my hotel and
dropped "Grand" from the name. However, for a brief moment,
I felt that my hotel retained its original title, Grand Hotel Des
Bains.

Alas, more than ten years ago I learned the hotel had closed
and was to be converted into a deluxe condominium complex
called the Residenze des Bains. Perhaps this venerable hotel
was not appreciated by the kinds of tourists who visit Venice
today. Rather than enjoy the charms of the various neighborhoods or appreciate the incredible works of art in its museums
and churches, they only spend a couple of nights in a famously
fancy hotel before boarding a behemoth of a cruise ship that
will deposit them briefly in Dubrovnik's town square or by a
windmill on the island of Mykonos. That crowd would not have
appreciated the glitter and gilt-free interiors of Des Bains.
Much too plain. Its closing was sad for me and those who rev-
eled in its elegant simplicity for over 120 years.

Today this building with its striking silhouette remains
along the shores of the Adriatic. In this hotel where Mann
wrote, Diaghilev died, and Gable slept while attending the 1935
Venice Film Festival, signs of neglect are everywhere. The interior has been vandalized, glorious Venetian glass chandeliers
have been stolen, and the exterior is crumbling. I fear that with
the coronavirus limiting travel, the Residenze will never reopen
and the property will eventually be demolished. Never again
will children race on the runners that were laid on those long
creaking upstairs halls. Diners will no longer enjoy the view

*Hotel Des Bains. Today,
the red carpet on the stairs
has been discarded.*

And the once active bar has been deserted.

through tall French doors, and after-dinner guests will no more hear the clinking of coffee cups, the tinkling of glasses, the wind rustling the pines, or the waves lapping on the shore. A grand old relic of the Venetian Gilded Age will be gone. Another Death in Venice.

KITTY

I STILL CANNOT FIGURE OUT HOW THAT SPARKLING, flower-filled Lucite cane left her hands and became an airborne missile hurling from the Dress Circle level of the Metropolitan Opera House to the orchestra level below. Greatly distressed, the cane's owner asked me if we should go down and retrieve it. I answered in the affirmative—the cane was decidedly distinctive looking, and so was its owner. We took a nearby elevator down to discover a more-than-middle-aged woman sitting on the floor, head in hands, our worst fears confirmed. When the wounded one recognized who it was that had crowned her from above, however, she did as close to a deep curtsy as one can manage from a sitting position and said, "Oh, Miss Carlisle, I saw you in *Río Rita* in 1932. It is such an honor meeting you." Such was the charisma of this Marx Brothers costarring, Met Opera singing, *To Tell the Truth* paneling, and New York State Council on the Arts chairing Kitty Carlisle Hart.

......

Kitty Carlisle Hart. Leading lady, singer, panelist,
and politician. Always a star.

I met Kitty due to the horrific Hurricane Agnes that in the summer of 1972 savaged the Southern Tier of New York State—the area just south of the Finger Lakes. At five in the morning, a five-foot wall of water crashed through the valley, which includes the small city of Corning and the corporate headquarters of what was then called Corning Glass Works, as well as the adjacent Corning Museum of Glass. This museum contained a priceless collection of glass as well as the library severely damaged in the storm. Worse yet, many of the employees' downtown houses were trashed, along with the main street, Market Street, and the antiquated downtown Baron Steuben Hotel. Kitty might have been staying there, along with the rest of the cast, since she was appearing that week at the playhouse in her late husband Moss Hart's play *Light Up the Sky.* It is tempting to paint a dramatic picture of Kitty, perfectly coiffed, sloshing through the rising water, patent-leather pumps in hand, headed toward higher ground. There would be waiting a dark-gray Bentley driven by John, the chauffeur, dispatched by Corning's Chairman Emeritus Amory Houghton, who lived with his wife, Laura, high up on the hill in their family house modestly named The Knoll. In fact, Kitty was already ensconced there, high and dry, as she was an old friend and had been invited to stay there for the duration of the play's run.

No such invitation was extended to me. Their youngest daughter, Meme, was married to me at the time and was staying at The Knoll with our children, Elizabeth and Andrew, and no invitation was required for me to join them and see how they

were faring. I took a 7 A.M. flight to Syracuse, the nearest airport open, and grabbed a cab to speed me to my destination.
Skirting the flooded valleys without the aid of GPS, I was de-
posited at the door of The Knoll. My unexpected arrival sur-

*The Knoll, Corning, New York. Home of the
Amory Houghton family, where Kitty took refuge during
the Agnes hurricane and flood of 1972.*

prised the assembled group having breakfast, including my family still in bathrobes and an elegant lady dressed in a pow-der-blue suit, two strands of pearls, and perfectly groomed hair crowning her smiling, welcoming face. That meeting with Kitty was a moment to remember.

The Agnes flood and its effect on the town of Corning was horrendous, but the bombing of the twin towers in New York City on September 11, 2001, left not a valley but a whole nation in a state of panic. People reacted to that unimaginable tragedy in very different ways. My thoughts turned to our Muslim

At the mosque, women were properly covered. Iranian-born Vida Belton wore her native costume.

neighbors in Carnegie Hill who were being harassed on the street and in stores, or so I was told. The second Sunday after the attack, I organized what I'd hoped would be a neighborly visit to the mosque on nearby 97th Street. I received enthusiastic support from members of various churches—St. James, Heavenly Rest, Brick, and a few others—as well as from civic groups like the Friends of the Upper East Side Historic Districts and CIVITAS. Our mission was to convince our neighbors that we most certainly did not blame them for the attacks and that we sympathized with their plight. The local police were alerted. The mosque's imam pledged to be nonpolitical. Finally, I asked Kitty if she would like to attend. I was not the least bit surprised when she enthusiastically agreed. I explained that her arms and head would have to be covered, but her famously beautiful legs could remain on view.

Sunday morning found her waiting in front of her apartment on East 63rd Street, and I was immediately aware that we had a problem. Her hair was elegantly covered by a beautiful Hermès silk scarf. No problem there, but her off-white silk blouse was inconveniently open, without necessary buttons to prevent an immodest exposure. Too shy to ask her to go upstairs and change, I desperately pulled at each end of the knotted scarf, hoping to better cover what most certainly would offend the good God-fearing folks who worshiped on East 97th Street. I hailed a taxi and, appropriately dressed or not, we headed north. Once inside the mosque, Kitty had to remove her black patent-leather pumps—no shoes in a mosque—while

I took a moment to down two Valiums before making my welcoming remarks. Suitably relaxed, I was halfway through my greetings when I saw Kitty wildly waving a sheet of paper at me from far across the room. The imam had double-crossed me and was distributing a paper saying that the destruction of the two towers was caused by Jews. What might have seemed laughable to me was not to the Jewish members of the audience, including Kitty, who was immediately concerned for the safety of her grandchildren. Thanks to the help of a media-wise friend, we discouraged the *Daily News,* which was covering the story, from publishing an article that would most certainly have featured Kitty, since she was the only really newsworthy person there. Her pumps retrieved, we hailed a taxi and returned Kitty to her apartment shaken, but safe and sound.

The last time I saw Kitty was less eventful. No flying missiles, no raging floods, and no terrible tragedy preceded our meeting. At the age of ninety-five, she was still doing what she called her "gigs," appearing at Feinstein's, singing some familiar songs and chatting about her famous friends. All very professional, including her voice, which was still strong and distinctive, her look smashing. She ended her performance with the song her very close friend Irving Berlin had written as a wedding present for his wife Ellin: "I'll Be Loving You, Always." Always Kitty.

At Feinstein's,
New York City,
on Kitty's ninety-
fourth birthday in
1972. She did her
last gigs there.

With Victor Gotbaum at my forty-fifth
birthday party on Ann Nitze's terrace.

TAXI

ONE OF THE JOYS OF ARRIVING AT LONDON'S
Heathrow Airport is to throw pounds not prunes to the wind
and take a London taxi into the city. There—unbelievably to
this New Yorker—you can find more-than-adequate legroom,
space for an entire family, and a driver who not only speaks
English but knows where you're going, be it the Ritz or a bed-
and-breakfast in Bayswater. The same driver can even deposit
you in front of a private club on St. James Street in the event
that you are that well connected. We had similar amenities in
New York years ago, but Checker cabs and homebred drivers
have vanished along with Ebbets Field, the Third Avenue El,
and Schrafft's. It is useless to compare the experience of riding
in one of those beloved cabs with today's hardly air-conditioned, head-hitting, leg-crunching, rattle-banging contrap-
tions. Even if your taxi is the one mandated by Mayor Bloomberg
and has more legroom, those newfangled cabs have platforms

......

*Top: Hydra, the port. Inset: The charioteer in the museum at Delphi.
Bottom: The valley of olives with the sea of Corinth beyond. Only a
few windmills were to be seen.*

so high and doors so unmanageable that mounting them requires Herculean strength, often unavailable to the elderly.

I was not worrying about the condition of my taxi when I
emerged one morning two summers ago from the Athens Plaza
hotel, located as close as possible to Greece's two finest, the
venerable Grande Bretagne and the slightly newer King
George—Athens's only truly grand hotels. In front, I easily
hailed a taxi to take me to the National Archaeological Museum, also Greece's finest. I was reasonably sure that my ride
would be comfortable since most of the taxis there are Mercedes. In fact, most of the cabs in Athens are German-made, as

Athens. Hotels Grand Bretagne, King George, and mine,
The Athens Plaza. As close to the GB as I can reasonably get.

well as those in Shanghai and, as far as I know, in Ouagadougou.
Greece possesses a marvelous highway system, but unlike most
of Europe it has never had a well-developed railroad system.
From that point of view, it is not ecologically advanced. However, surprisingly enough, in another way the Greeks are truly
involved in the fight to preserve our planet, as I discovered on
my last trip.

Greece's landscape includes mountains that cascade into
what Homer famously called the wine-dark sea. These mountains are mostly treeless, allowing the sun to cast a variety of
colorful shades throughout the day. I was surprised and more
than a little shocked to find slowly turning windmills atop a
very large percentage of these peaks. A road high up on the island of Evia is rated three Michelin stars for its spectacular
views, surprisingly as highly rated as the *Hermes of Praxiteles* and
indeed the Parthenon. I wonder if the experience of traveling
on this road will lose a star or two once the discerning publish-
ers in Paris discover that all those very mountains are topped
with those decidedly un-scenic windmills.

Those windmills certainly weren't there when I first traveled to Greece in the summer of 1959. I had splurged on a special deck-passage ticket that allowed me to sleep in solitary
splendor on the floor of the first-class deck on the *Marco Polo,*
which brought me from Venice to Piraeus. After graduating
from the Harvard Graduate School of Design, instead of taking
a year in Italy on a Fulbright scholarship as several of my classmates did, I decided to get a regular job working for a regular

architectural firm in Athens. I was soon taken up by a group of about forty kids my own age from Athens American College. They spoke in English all evening, even when chattering to one another, a gesture honoring not only me but my country. Such a gesture is unimaginable today because so many look at us with a mixture of contempt and pity for ever allowing Trump's corrupt and incompetent government to exist.

In that year the cha-cha was the dance of choice, and on many Saturday nights you could find me gyrating to its insistent beat at Greece's first disco, La Gudera, located on the picturesque port of the island of Hydra. When not dancing, we listened to the 45 rpm records of Nana Mouskouri, the Greek singer who was yet to find international fame with the song "Never on Sunday" that following year. On other weekends we all piled into the only car that any of us owned, a rattletrap bearing no resemblance to the aforementioned Mercedes taxis. Our destination was Delphi, or, to be exact, nearby Arachova, where the rooms and food were considerably cheaper. We all slept in one room, no pairing, as we had not yet been struck by the spirit of the free-loving 1960s. I was suitably impressed by the Temple of Apollo, the amphitheater, and the sublime *Charioteer of Delphi* statue in the museum. Most of all, I was in awe of the breathtaking view down to the valley filled with neat rows of thousands of olive trees and beyond that, in the distance, the dim, sparkling waters of the Gulf of Corinth.

In the summer of 2019 it was the memory of this view that inspired me to leave the mercifully undiscovered island of Evia

and motor up the high slopes of Mount Parnassus to the tour-
isty village of Delphi. Understandably, the Greeks are extremely
conscientious about preserving the beauty of their monuments
and landscapes. In Athens the buildings are kept low by law in
order to allow a view of the Parthenon from all parts of the city.
For that reason I was reasonably sure that I would not be out-

Top: The Goulandris Museum of Cycladic Art. Bottom: These
ancient figurines influenced many artists, including Picasso.

*Greek mountaintops are often crowned
by climate-conscious windmills.*

raged by the twin-kling lights of a newly erected water park on the distant shores of the Gulf of Corinth. But what about the ubiquitous windmills located on so many of their mountains? Gazing at these peaks from my well-placed balcony at the super-simple but strategically located Apollo Hotel, I could see a few slowly rotating blades, just a few, in the far, far distance. Relief spread through me as I opened a can of Fix beer from the mini bar and gazed at that long-remembered, awe-inspiring view.

Our excursion that day did not involve taking a taxi, as we had hired a poorly performing Peugeot that barely accomplished the extremely steep climb from Arachova to Delphi. This unfortunate French vehicle reminded me somewhat circuitously of those New York taxis. However, American cabs' deplorable state is also reflected in the condition of our roads, tunnels, bridges, airports, and health system—indeed, our approach to saving this planet. I can only marvel at the way tiny, perpetually insolvent Greece has attacked its energy problem by capping its mountains with windmills.

Although I dwell occasionally on the earth's destruction, far more often my concerns are more pedestrian, like the single lane that is the only one usable on Lexington Avenue, the construction sheds on so many buildings on Park Avenue, the continuing use of pennies that stalls checkout lines, and, of course, the condition of those high-riding New York taxis. I long to be in the Athenian taxi that once found me cruising up one of Athens's few truly broad grand avenues, Vasilissis Sofias, on my way to see the ravishing icons in the Benaki Museum and the timeless pre-Minoan statues in the Goulandris Museum of Cycladic Art, long my favorite. Stretching my legs, I would lean back and enjoy riding in a perfectly quiet, smooth, air-conditioned taxi.

A Tesla New York taxi. These new ones are less grand than the Athenian taxis, but better for the environment.

DEAR DAVID

THERE ARE MANY THINGS I WISH I HAD MASTERED
in those musty classrooms in the ancient building on West 77th
Street that housed the Collegiate School. For one, I would like
to have mastered the art of French conversation, and for another paid more attention to the American authors Emily
Dickinson and Edith Wharton. On a more pedestrian level, I
regret that I never learned to type, a skill so necessary in our
laptop-laden world. One thing I did learn early on was the
proper, simple, straightforward way to begin a letter. Whether
it be to your best friend, an acquaintance, or a stranger, you begin
by writing *Dear* someone: Dear Mr. Emery, Dear William, or
Dear Bill. Easy. To my great dismay, *Dear* has been replaced by the
universally used *Hi* even if the letter is to a total stranger.

Why the change in the use of this simple, time-honored
salutation? I have a terrible feeling that in our "me too" world,

......

*Jeremiah Smith Hall, Phillips Exeter Academy. Where the boys
waited for mail from home—and from girls.*

On occasion, girls were invited to visit the all-male
academy. Some came from Farmington.

people may think that writing *Dear* implies that you are angling
for a more intimate relationship, in fact, a hookup. On the other
hand, *Hi* seems too casual a greeting when extended by an eager
salesman trying to persuade you to hand over your meager life
savings to a broker at Merrill Lynch. Certainly beginning a Dear
John letter with *Hi* seems like a somewhat insensitive way of
saying goodbye.

In days gone by, there was a proper way of starting a correspondence, the aforementioned *Dear,* but closing was open to a
variety of choices. My schoolteacher gave me the options of
ending with *Sincerely,* most commonly, or *Very truly yours,* perhaps a bit more formal. *Best regards* seemed a bit more friendly
and *Fondly,* friendlier still. To me, ending a letter with *Love* or
more emphatically *Much love* was used with caution, for it de-

noted that the person was enjoying a very special, very close relationship, usually agreed to by both consenting parties.

The thought of ending a letter with *Love* reminds me that during my last two years of boarding school the mail arrived at about 11 A.M. on the first floor of Jeremiah Smith Hall at Phillips Exeter Academy and found me waiting in great anticipation for a letter from a very special young woman. I had met her at my father's twenty-fifth reunion at Harvard. We began talking on a hired bus bound for Singing Beach on the North Shore, an outing arranged for the families of the reunion-goers. Later we saw a bit of each other, and wrote fairly frequently. It was in my senior year after she had come up for the weekend's winter dance that we started ending our letters with *Love*. Today this would be like a declaration to the world that we were boyfriend and girlfriend. Earthshaking. Oh how I anticipated those dark-blue envelopes with the neatly written return address on the back from Farmington, Connecticut! In the end neither God nor nature intended me to enjoy exactly that kind of sustained relationship with a girl. And so it ended, but with the golden haze of time clouding my memory, I remember the days of writing *Love* with enormous far-felt pleasure.

Those letters on dark-blue paper were handwritten, as were mine. In fact, I never learned to type at Exeter, and as a result today I must hunt and peck my way through my emails, a laborious procedure. The all-wise masters at Exeter obviously assumed that if I had any later need for correspondence, it would be handled by a female secretary often as not trained at Katharine Gibbs. I envy my furiously fingering friends as they tap out messages at astonishing rates and I only wish that my voluminous, lengthy missives resulted in equally lengthy responses. Their one-line notes are peppered with *u*'s, *c*'s, *lols*, and perhaps a closing *xx, xox,* or even *xoxox.* As things are, I'm resigned to short cryptic responses.

I'm slowly crawling into the twenty-first century, but I still on more than a few occasions say *icebox* instead of *refrigerator* and *drugstore* instead of *pharmacy.* I'm sure few people notice

Central Park South. For better or worse, the Dubai-ing of New York has changed our skyline drastically.

that I still walk on the street side when escorting a lady friend, and not surprisingly women look puzzled when I take my hat off in an elevator. Prehistoric maybe, but it's hard to ignore such an ingrained habit. I've learned to wear white sneakers with my black pants, gaining at least the approval of my with-it son-in-law, Brian. I am no longer surprised when a young friend says that I have "crushed" something when I have been deemed successful. I'm addicted to using my iPhone to keep up with family and friends on Facebook and—more important—Instagram, appar-

ently preferred by the young. After many more than a hundred calls from "New York, NY," offering me a zero-interest credit line, I have reluctantly given up my landline—so fondly remembered from the Regent 4 Butterfield 8 days. Sadly, I have been reduced, not even to a 917, but to an ignominious 347.

I have even stopped snarling at the Dubai-ing of the Central Park South skyline, with its parade of preening pencil-like towers. As I pause to rest at the top of the Great Lawn on my biweekly walks in the park, I am now slightly dazzled by the audacity of it all. That said, I still wish that friends and perhaps even foes would start their correspondence to me with the once universally accepted, totally noncommittal, time-tested *Dear David.*

TAVERNA

THE CEILING FANS THAT REVOLVED LAZILY ABOVE us in a sparsely occupied café in Kolonaki Square hardly mitigated the midday heat of Athens in August. Most of those who lived nearby in this upscale neighborhood had fled town for a nearby beach resort or for a more distant island. At that moment my then partner, later husband, Tyree and I decided that we wanted to leave, too, but for where? Both of us had spent time on the island of Santorini in past years. In the mid-1950s I had spent almost a week there sketching the jumble of white-walled houses that clung to the cliffs. One day I walked down a dirt path to the beach and discovered that wearing a bathing suit was unnecessary since I was the only visitor that day. Alas, that same beach is now bordered by dozens of restaurants, condos, hotels, and even an airfield.

......

The Apollon Suites Hotel on Evia, the Greek island least visited by foreigners—and now tragically famous for its devastating fires, fortunately far from this hotel. Inset: Tyree relaxes at our nearby taverna.

Tyree's time there extended over a two-year period while he was a part-time caretaker of a house in the main town of Thira. He was able to enjoy the white-walled, bougainvillea-covered buildings long before camera-carrying refugees from the cruise ships clogged the steep alleys almost year-round. We had experienced the island's best years. It was time to move on. As we sat sipping a Fix beer under those slowly whirling fans, I noticed a map of Greece printed on the paper mat that half covered the table before me. Looking at it, I spied a crescent-shaped area on the south tip of the island of Evia, very close to Athens on the north side. Might that south-facing crescent-shaped piece of land contain a beach? And just maybe a nice nearby hotel? It was worth a try.

The next morning, suitcases in hand, we boarded a ferry and in less than two hours rounded a narrow spit of land and spotted a white sandy beach, adjacent to the town of Karystos. On the quay, there was a sign encouraging us to walk eight hundred meters to a hotel named the Apollon Suites Hotel. At the end of our trek, we were faced with an undistinguished five-story tower, not the quaint cottage colony cluster that I had envisioned. Once inside, however, I discovered a flagstone floor that led past an almost completely open wall to a lawn, an umbrella-strewn beach, and the sun-dappled sea beyond. We were home.

Going into town that evening, we found a place totally devoid of the bougainvillea-covered walls. In fact, there was nothing remotely picturesque to attract the camera-carrying set. In the eve-

The Apollon Suites Hotel beach. Tyree was
a great swimmer, me not so much.

ning men side by side with men, and women arm in arm with other women, paraded along the quay, very much as they had when I first visited Amalfi in 1951. Back then the flickering lights of fishing boats twinkled on the horizon. There, as here, overfishing has diminished the seafood trade almost to the point of nothingness. Once I did order fish in one of the quayside restaurants, only to discover that it cost slightly more than it would for family and friends at Estiatorio Milos on West 55th Street.

Our first meals in Karystos, cooked to order, were not special. Later we discovered a simple taverna just up the hill from

our hotel that served precooked food at almost room tempera-
ture from pots and platters in the kitchen. Customers would get
up from the table and inspect the falling-off-the-bone roast
chicken and baby lamb, lemon potatoes, beans in oil, and, my
favorite, ripe red tomatoes stuffed with rice and small bits of
lamb. A single row of tables lined the terrace, a narrow, little-
used road and a hut with the kitchen on one side, a low fence
and the sea below on the other. In the early afternoon the sun
brightened the pines that clung to the steep hill above and sea

below. The occasional raised voice of one of the few patrons was the only noise, except for the soft humming of crickets and the gentle lapping of the sea. It is one of the most peaceful places I have ever known.

Tyree loved this taverna. He often told me he would like to have his ashes scattered in the Aegean. What better place than the sea below the taverna where we had sipped glasses of local white wine, smelled the pines, listened to the crickets, and stared at the blue-green sea, hardly saying a word. At peace.

A nearby taverna. Quite perfect. One of the great places in the world for lunch.

A WHITE-BRICK
BUILDING

A LMOST EIGHTY BLOCKS SEPARATED MY PARENTS'
apartment from the house where my grandparents lived before
the war. Most Sundays I bridged the distance by taking a Fifth
Avenue double-decker bus—sometimes, most happily, open—
from the West Village to their home at 51 East 74th Street. This
house had five stories, and yet it could not accurately be de-
scribed as a town house. *Town house* denotes a singular structure,
most often clad in limestone, whereas their home was part of a
string of identical brick-clad buildings distinguished only by
the fact that Eleanor Roosevelt had lived in one of them during
her last years of life. In the Village we lived in a duplex in a
four-story walk-up on one side of the Bleecker Gardens, a com-
munal open space that we shared with neighbors who included

......

On East 90th Street. The garden terrace on the 14th floor,
a demi-paradise.

*The garden terrace. A broad awning allows for lunches,
even in midsummer.*

Mark Van Doren, the writer and poet whose son famously cheated on the quiz show *Twenty-One*. During the war my father worked for the War Production Board in Washington, and we lived in bucolic simplicity in a modest white house with green blinds in a densely wooded, secluded area of Bethesda. War over, we moved back to the city and lived at 75th and Park. My mother, who considered herself very progressive, always apologized for living on Park Avenue, though, as she admitted, we enjoyed high ceilings, a fireplace in the living room, a separate dining room, and two maids' rooms ideal for growing boys.

When I went to Harvard, I shared a suite of rooms in Eliot House that boasted not only a fireplace but also a sweeping view of the Charles River. Once we married, in 1962, Meme and I avoided the usual middle move for young marrieds and found an extraordinary duplex apartment, for an exceedingly reasonable price, at the landmarked 131 East 66th Street. This apartment was low on bedrooms but high on living spaces, which included a two-story living room and a library both with fireplaces, a dining room, and a kitchen where, peculiarly, the service elevator opened directly. Tons of charm! Tons of class! Simple or grand, that's the way my family and my friends lived, always with "class."

After all these character-filled domiciles it may surprise you to learn that I have spent almost half of my lifetime in an apartment house that has absolutely no character, no charm, and certainly no class whatsoever. I live in a white-brick building. Such buildings were built after the Second World War and until

quite recently. Their light-colored exteriors vaguely imitate the
great apartment house designed by Le Corbusier, Unité d'Habi-
tation in Marseille. They have mostly eight-foot ceilings, no
fireplaces, no service elevators, laundries in the basement, small
baths, and small kitchens. In my youth I visited one such building belonging to my long-suffering, mostly neglected piano
teacher. Any attempt to make these apartments look fancy ends
up making them look ridiculous. In one department, however,
my white-brick building could not be more classy, comparing
favorably with the service at 720 Park and 834 Fifth: the staff.
At my advanced age, I need a considerable amount of help, and
my many needs, including some of the maintenance of my tree-
filled terrace garden, are tended to. Owners of grand six-story
limestone-clad but superintendent-less town houses are allowed to eat their hearts out.

I love my characterless white brick building. I could say
with great pretentiousness that I am living between Park and
Lexington, where the entrance is, but the tower is most definitely on Lexington Avenue. Yes, I live on Lexington Avenue,
and over a store at that. Mixed use, I call it. When I first moved
in, I told my friends that I lived in a junior four over Gristedes.
This is no longer an apt description since I now have a somewhat larger apartment and the retail space below is suddenly
vacant, a victim of the coronavirus.

Miraculously, much of Lexington Avenue in my immediate
area is still thriving, despite the virus. One block in each direc-
tion, I have a newly transplanted Gristedes, a cleaner, a health

food store, a women's hairdresser, a sandwich and bakery shop, a liquor store, a woman's day spa, a pizza parlor, a seriously talented picture framer, a Chinese take-out restaurant, a barbershop, a jewelry store interestingly paired with a shoe repair shop, even a smoke shop(!)—and, in the middle of it all, a genuine local neighborhood eatery, Lex Restaurant. It remains a somewhat Italian, very hospitable place for families, couples, and most important singles. Also, it serves the 92nd Street Y, two blocks up, on Lexington Avenue. Baked lasagna and a glass of Chianti before Thomas L. Friedman or the Emerson String Quartet.

For many years my fondness for locally owned shops led me to scorn the presence of larger chain stores and banks. Now, as I endure certain mobility problems, I am exceedingly glad that my Chase banker is only a block away on Third Avenue. He soothes my distress when I confess that I've lost my ATM card, again. Years back, no one was more distressed than I when the perfectly marvelous hardware store closed a block away. It sold all of the expected stuff, but also colorful paper plates, wineglasses of every variety, even Christmas ornaments. I have somewhat reluctantly entered the twenty-first century now, and when my iPhone refuses to send me any messages from either friends or foes I am mightily happy having Jose waiting behind his pink-hued storefront to get me back online.

Remembering the charm-filled abodes I inhabited formerly, I occasionally envy my friends who live in The Beresford on Central Park West. They enjoy high ceilings, fireplaces, views

of the Jacqueline Kennedy Onassis Reservoir, and the possibility of hobnobbing with neighbors Barbara Walters, Paul Gold-
berger, Betsy Gotbaum—and in past days the late Beverly Sills.
I imagine that evenings spent with that crowd would be slightly
more elevating than those with my Lex Restaurant group, jolly
as they are. Then I remember how convenient it was to live
over Duane Reade and how, if I lived next to Barbara and Betsy, instead of dropping downstairs to
buy much-needed cough syrup, I would have to
trudge a very long, windy West Side block only to
find two stores, Bicycle Renaissance and Patago-
nia, neither carrying baby aspirin. Other stores
nearby are trendy clothing shops, all useless.

At East 90th Street I've always enjoyed the vi-
brant neighborhood outside my door, but my original junior four faced north, depriving me of direct
sunlight; although serviceable and spacious enough
for a solitary soul, it lacked the charm of my previ-
ous abodes. A south-facing apartment became
available on a high floor and I ignored its low ceiling and lack of a fireplace. Outbidding the competition, I bought it. With the invaluable help of
Michael Walter, garden designer and owner of
Lexington Gardens, we created on its large terrace
a demi-paradise of shrubs and flowering bushes,
evergreens and maples, plain and Japanese, wa-
tered almost nightly by me, a most unlikely gar-

dener. I enjoy the cooling breezes, the summer sunsets, and the warming rays during the spring and fall at lunchtime, all the while living in Carnegie Hill. No need to take a Jitney to Bridge-hampton.

When the coronavirus came in 2020, shutting down the city, a ghostly hush descended over my neighborhood. With

Lex Restaurant with Skippy presiding. Outdoor dining at this nearby neighborhood restaurant, and it's here to stay.

little traffic noise, I could hear a bird chirping from the top of one of the red maples at the far end of my terrace. I am grateful that I can open my doors and walk into my still-blooming

garden far above Lexington Avenue, sequestered but alive and safe. Indeed, I am almost happy and feel most lucky to be in a white-brick building.

The garden terrace. The superbly designed planting is by Michael Walter at Lexington Gardens, and requires my watering it almost every day.

EPILOGUE

I THINK WE ALL HAVE SOME DRAWERS WHERE WE CRAM photos of family times together and trips long-ago taken to places happily remembered. I have a couple of such drawers. So when the photo editor for this book asked me for some specific shots, I found dozens and dozens of pictures taken in Greece, Venice, and other European sites; many more of China; some even of the marches we took for causes we believed in. Deep in the drawer I found a letter written in a familiar handwriting and read it.

It was written when Tyree was in London, where he was studying acting technique at LAMDA. Before that he had taken classes with Jerzy Grotowski in Krakow and Stella Adler in New York. Tyree had many parts in off-off-Broadway plays—more than one a year. He was always hoping to gain work in more important companies but always suffering rejections. Finally he played the lead in a production that ran for two weeks

......

Tyree Giroux. Actor, theater professional, world traveler, and the most caring friend that Nuala, Orla, and Ona will ever have.

*Above: Tyree
in China.*

*Right: Card sent
from Tyree in
London on the
day of Charles
and Diana's
marriage.*

at the 59 East 59th Street Playhouse, where his acting skills and his truly remarkable voice could be appreciated.

The letter told me that it was raining, and that he was going out to have a pint in Chelsea at the King's Head and Eight Bells on the Thames before ending the day at the nearby Tate Gallery. He also told me that he was lonely, that he missed me, and that he loved me, too. Now, we were together for thirty-nine years, married for less than one, and neither of us very often expressed affection. More strongly than ever I realized that the life we had together—going to the theater and the opera, flying to Europe for special exhibitions, having a pint in a pub on the Thames, or a lunch in a shady Shanghai garden—would never happen again. To him, and to the times we had together and the people he charmed, I dedicate these pieces of the past.

Tyree and David. Partners for thirty-nine years, married for less than a year.

ACKNOWLEDGMENTS

. . .

Pieces of the Past WOULD NOT HAVE BEEN POSSIBLE without the dedicated assistance of Kris Monroe. With great patience, he transcribed my long legal pad scribbles into a workable manuscript as together we pondered word choices and ways of expression. Transforming our efforts into this book took the professional and organizational skills of my editor Maggie Simmons and her superlative team. Many thanks to creative director Barbara Bachman for her beautiful and imaginative design and to photo editor Laurie Winfrey, who made excellent and arresting choices among the many images we considered. I also want to acknowledge copyeditor Laura Jorstad, who gave keen attention to stylistic and factual issues. Finally, as luck and life would have it, I was able to avail myself of the counsel of writer and editor Michael Korda. I am grateful for his assistance.

PHOTO CREDITS

...

. . .

DAVID W. BEER is a native New Yorker who has lived most of his adult life on his beloved Lexington Avenue, first with his wife and two children on 66th Street, and now on his own a little farther up on 90th Street.

He was educated at Harvard College and the Harvard Graduate School of Design before he embarked on his long and distinguished architectural career.

For years he was the director of design for Welton Becket, New York, a large international firm. There he designed headquarters buildings for many corporate clients, including the Mellon Bank in Pittsburgh, Barclays Bank International at 75 Wall Street, and more.

Later Beer formed his own firm with partners Henry Brennan, Peter Gorman, and Julia Monk. Designing hotels was a major part of his work, among them the Mandarin Oriental, the W Union Square, and the total renovation of the St. Regis, all in New York City. In Asia, he designed the Peninsulas in Bangkok and Shanghai. Beer's projects spanned the world, from Iran to Russia, Congo, Indonesia, and China, reinforcing a love of travel and adventure inculcated in him from an early age by his family.

With his amazing memory for people and places, eye for detail, good humor, and huge joie de vivre, Beer has now captured all of it in this book—a dazzling collection of picture postcards from a life well lived.